W9-AWT-061

International Food Library

FOOD IN
SPAIN

International Food Library

FOOD IN
SPAIN

text by
Nancy Loewen

recipes compiled by
Judith A. Ahlstrom

Rourke Publications, Inc.
Vero Beach, Florida 32964

Library of Congress Cataloging-in-Publication Data

Loewen, Nancy, 1964-
 Food in Spain / by Nancy Loewen
  p. cm. — (International food library)
 Includes bibliographical references and index.
 Summary: Describes the food products, cooking and eating customs, and festivals of Spain.
 ISBN 0-86625-346-7
 1. Cookery, Spanish—Juvenile literature. 2. Spain—Social life and customs—1951—Juvenile literature. [1. Cookery, Spanish. 2. Spain—Social life and customs.] I. Title. II. Series.
TX723.5.S7L64   1991
641.5946—dc20   90-43595
                                                            CIP
PRINTED IN THE USA   AC

CONTENTS

AN INTRODUCTION TO SPAIN

In a public square, red-and-white-clad Spaniards dance gaily to the music of guitars and castanets.

Sheep and goats peacefully graze the plains on a summer evening. On a nearby hill, an ancient castle seems to watch over them.

With thousands of people cheering in the stands, a matador dramatically waves his cape before a charging bull.

All of these images, and many more, have long been associated with the country of Spain. Located in the southwest corner of Europe, Spain lies between the Atlantic Ocean and the Mediterranean Sea. It covers nearly five-sixths of the Iberian Peninsula. (Portugal occupies the rest of the peninsula.) The southern tip of Spain is just eight miles from the continent of Africa, across the Strait of Gibraltar. In the northeast, Spain shares a border with France.

Narrow, sloping streets are part of the scenery in the Spanish city of Granada.

Spain is the third largest country in Europe—only the Soviet Union and France are bigger. Two island groups are also part of Spain: the Balearic Islands, found 50 to 150 miles east of mainland Spain in the Mediterranean Sea, and the Canary Islands, located off the northwest coast of Africa in the Atlantic Ocean.

Spain is known for its hot, dry summers and cold winters. There are regions with a very different climate, however. Winds from the Atlantic Ocean bring moderate temperatures and much precipitation to the mountainous region of northern Spain. Along the Mediterranean Coast, the winters are mild and often rainy.

The population of Spain is about 39 million people. Nearly 10 percent of the people live in the capital city of Madrid. Other important cities include Barcelona, Valencia, and Seville.

7

SPAIN'S HISTORY & GOVERNMENT

Spain has a long and varied history. In ancient times, such peoples as the Carthaginians, Visigoths, and Romans fought over Spain. Many Roman aqueducts and bridges still remain from that period.

The Moors controlled Spain beginning in the 700's A.D. The Moors were originally from North Africa. They were Muslims, having been converted to the religion of Islam by invading Arabs. In the centuries that they occupied the Iberian Peninsula, the Moors greatly advanced Spanish culture. They were skilled farmers, and also emphasized education and the arts. Like the Romans, they, too, left their mark on the landscape. *Mosques* (places of worship) and fortified palaces called *alcázars* dot the Spanish countryside.

The Alhambra in Granada was a palace for Moorish kings. This is one of the many gardens on the grounds.

When the Christians took control of Spain, they began to build cathedrals. Most, like this one, were built in the "gothic" style.

Christian kingdoms began driving out the Moors in the eleventh century, but didn't succeed completely until 1492—the same year Christopher Columbus discovered America. By this time, most of Spain was united under the rule of King Ferdinand and Queen Isabella. An exciting age of exploration and conquest soon began. In the early 1800's, however, wars and economic problems caused Spain to lose most of its great empire. It became a poor country, and remained that way until the mid-20th century, when an industrial boom took place.

After the death of dictator Francisco Franco in 1975, the people of Spain formed a democratic government. The king (or queen) serves as head of state, and represents Spain at ceremonial events. However, it is the prime minister who is responsible for most of the day-to-day workings of the national government. The prime minister is the leader of the political party that has the most members in the parliament.

Juan Carlos I became king of Spain in 1975, and still holds that title. As of 1990, Felipe González Márquez is the prime minister. He leads the Socialist Workers' Party.

9

AGRICULTURE & INDUSTRY IN SPAIN

Much of Spain consists of a high plateau called the Meseta. The poor soil of the Meseta and Spain's generally dry climate are long-standing challenges to Spanish farmers. More and more, farmers depend on irrigation and modern farming techniques to grow their crops.

Crops grown in northern Spain include barley, potatoes, and wheat. In southern and eastern Spain, wine grapes, olives, oranges, and lemons are the major crops. Bananas are grown on the Canary Islands, while grapes and olives are the most important crops on the Balearic island of Majorca.

Sheep graze on the grassy highlands of the Meseta, and their wool is another important product. Spanish farmers also raise beef and dairy cattle, goats, chickens, and pigs.

Grapes are an important crop. Spain is the fourth-leading wine producer in the world.

Large orchards of oranges, lemons, and other fruits are a common sight around Valencia, a city on the eastern coast of Spain.

Surrounded by water, Spain is one of Europe's most important fishing countries. Most of the fishing takes place off Spain's northern coast, where anchovies, cod, hake, octopus, sardines, squid, and tuna are caught.

Before 1950, nearly half of all Spanish workers were involved with agriculture or fishing. Then a great industrial boom took place. People moved to the cities to take jobs in manufacturing, mining, construction, and other industries. Today, most people live in cities, and agriculture and fishing employ less than 22 percent of Spanish workers. Even most farmers live in villages, rather than in homes on their land.

Spain is one of the world's largest producers of automobiles. Other products include textiles, plastics, electronic equipment, cement, steel, and iron. Tourism is another important industry, employing one out of every 10 Spaniards. Spain's sunny Mediterranean coast, colorful fiestas, and ancient castles attract up to 40 million visitors each year!

11

FIESTA!

Each July thousands of people gather in Pamplona for the fiesta, or festival, of San Fermin. For 10 days, tourists and Spaniards alike take part in parades, dancing, drinking, and watching bullfights. The most dramatic event, however, is "the running of the bulls." Each morning the bulls are run through the streets of Pamplona to the bullring, with the young people of the city running just ahead of them. The idea is to stay as close to the bulls as possible, without getting hurt. It's a time-honored tradition—and one best left to those who know what they are doing!

The fiesta of San Fermin, which is held in honor of the town's patron saint, is probably the best-known Spanish celebration, but there are plenty of others. In fact, just about every town holds a summer festival in which a local patron saint is honored. Spain's population is close to 90 percent Roman Catholic, so it's natural that many Spanish festivals have a religious connection.

Spanish fiestas are colorful events, often involving traditional costumes and dances.

A religious procession winds its way through the streets of Toledo during Holy Week.

During Holy Week—the week before Easter—many cities hold solemn parades. Floats made to represent Christ or the Virgin Mary are drawn through the streets. Drumbeats or wailing religious songs accompany the procession. All across Spain, people decorate their balconies with specially blessed palm branches.

The city of Valencia has an interesting celebration called *fallas*, held in March. This tradition began in medieval times, when, once a year, carpenters burned their wood scraps and shavings in enormous bonfires. Today, instead of burning wood scraps, people burn representations of local leaders or celebrities—made just for the occasion.

Dancing and music are always a delightful part of any Spanish celebration. During the fiesta of San Fermín, the bands play until four in the morning! Each region has its own favorite dances and songs. Some of these dances, such as the *flamenco* and the *bolero*, have become famous throughout the world.

THE SPANISH BULLFIGHT

To many people, the drama of the bullfight is what Spain is all about. The bullfighting season lasts from March to October, with fights taking place on Sunday afternoons. The *matador*, or person who kills the bull, is the star of the event. Many other people have roles as well.

In the first part of a bullfight, the animal is set free into the ring. The matador waves his cape at the bull to attract it. He then ducks away so he can study the bull's reactions. Soon the matador remains in the ring with the bull, each wave of his cape more dramatic than the last as the bull thunders by.

Bullfighting draws large crowds during a fiesta, such as this celebration in Málaga.

In what is known as
"the moment of truth,"
the matador thrusts his
sword into the bull.

Next, bullfighters called *picadores* enter the ring, riding horses and carrying spears. Their job is to try to weaken the large muscle on the top of the bull's neck. After this, people called *banderilleros* plant decorated darts in the bull's shoulders. By now the bull is in a weakened state.

Now they are ready for the kill. Instead of a large cape, the matador waves a small red cloth in front of the bull. His sword is ready. He must kill the bull at just the right moment. The bull's front feet must be together, and its head must be at a low angle. Only then will the matador be able to kill the bull quickly and cleanly as he thrusts his sword between the bull's shoulders.

This process is usually repeated six times during a bullfight, which can last up to three hours. Three matadors kill two bulls each. A matador who performs well is awarded the bull's ear. If it is an outstanding performance, the matador may be awarded both ears, or even the ears and the tail.

Bullfighting isn't as popular as it once was. Both in Spain and elsewhere, animal-rights groups are working to bring an end to this sport. For now, however, the bullfight remains a part of Spanish tradition.

SOME SPANISH CUSTOMS

The *siesta*, or afternoon rest, is one of Spain's best-known customs. Throughout the country, shops, businesses, factories, churches, and other public places are shut down for two or three hours each afternoon. Spaniards return to their homes and enjoy an unhurried lunch with their families or friends. If there's enough time, they may take a nap before returning to their jobs.

Especially during the summer, the siesta is a very good idea. It's a way to keep people out of the hot sun! Like bullfighting, however, the siesta is not as widely practiced as it once was.

During the siesta, city streets are almost empty. At other times, however, they can be very busy—this outdoor market provides everything from vegetables to clothing.

Tapas, or appetizers, are a fun tradition in Spanish cafés and bars. Above are fresh mushrooms stuffed with ham.

Another tradition—the *paseo,* or evening walk—is as popular as ever. In the early part of the evening, after the stores are closed, Spaniards put on their nicest clothes and stroll through the streets. They may stop to chat with their friends and neighbors, or perhaps order a drink at a sidewalk café or bar. Afterwards, around 10:30 or so, they will eat a late dinner, either at home or at a restaurant. Most Spaniards eat out quite often, and there are usually lots of good restaurants from which to choose.

In any Spanish bar or café, one is sure to find *tapas*—small, tasty tidbits of food. Tapas may be pieces of fried fish or shellfish, marinated cubes of beef or seafood, olives, ham, deviled eggs, or other treats. Each place has its own specialty. Sometimes, instead of eating dinner, Spaniards and tourists will go from one bar or café to another, eating tapas along the way!

Lunch is traditionally the main meal of the day in Spain. Breakfast is very small, often not much more than a roll and cup of coffee, if that. Dinner, too, is light, perhaps a salad and a slice of *omelette.* Wine is served with both lunch and dinner.

COOKING IN SPAIN

Fresh seafood is a staple of many Spanish meals. One of the most popular dishes is *paella*. In this recipe, saffron-seasoned rice is combined with small chunks of seafood and meat. This is topped with green peas, crayfish, and red pimento. Paella is most often served at lunch, and it is usually cooked and served in a shallow iron pan.

Gazpacho is another common Spanish dish. This is a cold soup made from tomatoes, olive oil, and vinegar. Bread cubes, chopped cucumbers, or green peppers may accompany it. Gazpacho makes a refreshing meal in warm weather. Another way to cool down is with a popular Spanish beverage called *sangría*. It is made from wine, soda water, fruit, and fruit juice.

Pil-pil is a dish that is popular along the northern coast of Spain. It is made by slowly cooking salt codfish in olive oil.

Roast meats are a
specialty in Castile,
a region in northern
Spain.

Desserts aren't given as much attention in Spain as in other European countries, but there are plenty of Spanish favorites. *Polvorones* are dry, sweet cakes that come from Spain's Moorish heritage. *Flan* is a type of caramel custard. Other dessert choices include fresh fruit, or perhaps ice cream flavored with almonds, hazelnuts, or rum and raisins. During fiestas, stands are set up to sell *churros*, strips of dough that are deep-fried and sprinkled with sugar.

Spanish cooking includes countless regional specialties. Baby eel, cooked with olive oil, garlic, and peppers, is a local luxury in the Basque country of north central Spain. Castile is known for its roast meats, such as suckling pig or lamb. In Catalonia, *pasta* dishes and snails are common, as is a strong relish made with garlic. Whatever the dish, olive oil and garlic are two of the most common ingredients.

A FESTIVE MEAL

Shrimp Cocktail
Valencian Salad
Paella
Your choice of vegetable
Flan with Caramel Sauce

Paella and other seafood dishes are very common in Spain, a land surrounded by oceans. Each course in this festive meal should be served separately, except for the vegetable, which should be served with the main course (the paella).

Shrimp Cocktail

24 large shrimp, cooked or raw
cocktail sauce (see recipe below)

1. If raw shrimp are used, bring a pot of lightly salted water to a boil. Add the shrimp and cook 4–5 minutes on medium heat. The shrimp will turn pink when done.
2. Rinse the shrimp in a colander with cold water. Remove the shrimp shells and chill for 1 hour longer.
3. Arrange shrimp in individual serving dishes. Pour cocktail sauce over each serving. Garnish with lemon wedges. Serves 4–6.

Cocktail Sauce

1 ¼ cups mayonnaise
2 tablespoons tomato paste
1 tablespoon lemon juice
1 teaspoon grated lemon rind
add garlic powder, salt, and pepper to taste

1. Mix all ingredients in a small bowl. Chill 1 hour or longer. Serve with shrimp.

Shrimp Cocktail

Valencian Salad

> 2 sweet red bell peppers
> 1 tablespoon sliced green olives
> 1 large head of lettuce
> 3 oranges
> 1 clove garlic
> 2 yolks from hard-boiled eggs (discard whites)
> $1/4$ teaspoon black pepper
> 5 tablespoons olive oil
> 2 tablespoons wine vinegar
> 1 pinch sugar
> 4 ounces sour cream ($1/4$ cup)

1. Slice the peppers (remove seeds) and the oranges (remove peel). Wash the lettuce and allow it to dry.
2. Rub the bowl with the garlic clove, then add pepper slices, lettuce, olives, and oranges.
3. In a bowl, mash the egg yolks with a fork. Stir in the pepper, oil, and vinegar. Finally, stir in the sugar and sour cream. Pour this over the salad, toss, and serve. Serves 4–6.

Paella

Paella

    12 large shrimp or prawns, shelled
    12 mussels or clams
    2 cups long grain rice
    2 cups olive oil
    2 cups chopped onion
    4 cloves garlic, chopped
    2 tomatoes, chopped
    1 1/2 pounds cut-up cooked chicken
    1/2 teaspoon each: salt, paprika, pepper, marjoram
    2 tablespoons fresh parsley, chopped
    1 tablespoon lemon juice
    3/4 cup sliced green olives
    1 cup red, green, or yellow bell pepper, cut into strips
    1 cup frozen green peas, thawed

1. Wash and dry the shrimp, then sauté in butter until pink. Set aside but keep warm. Scrub the mussels, then steam in 1/4 cup of water until they open (about 5 minutes). Set aside and keep warm.
2. Cook rice about 10 minutes in 4 cups water; drain.
3. Heat the oil in a large pan and then add onion, garlic, tomatoes, and chicken. Mix well and cook until lightly browned. Add the cooked rice and half of the shrimp. Stir well so that everything is coated with oil. Cook about 20 minutes.
4. Stir in salt, paprika, pepper, marjoram, thyme, parsley, lemon juice, olive slices, peas, and pepper strips. Cook about 10 minutes longer.
5. Garnish top with remaining shrimp and the mussels. Serve in the pan. Serves 6.

Flan

> 4 eggs, beaten slightly
> 1/4 cup sugar
> 1/2 teaspoon salt
> 1 quart milk (4 cups)
> 1 teaspoon vanilla extract
> nutmeg
> caramel sauce (see recipe below)

1. Heat the milk in a saucepan on medium heat for about 10 minutes, stirring frequently. *Do not boil!*
2. In a large bowl, beat the eggs slightly, add the sugar and salt, and stir until well mixed. Add the hot milk slowly, stirring constantly. Finally stir in the vanilla and a little nutmeg. Mix thoroughly.
3. Grease 6–8 custard cups or a 1½-quart casserole and fill with the custard mixture. Place cups or casserole in a shallow pan containing warm water. Bake at 325°: 45 minutes for individual custards, or 50–60 minutes for a large custard.
4. Test for doneness by inserting a knife into the center of the custard. If the knife comes out clean, the custard is done. Chill well, then unmold the custard by setting in warm water for a few seconds and tipping upside down on a plate. Pour caramel sauce over the custard. Serves 6–8.

Caramel Sauce

> 2 cups sugar
> 1 cup boiling water
> 1/8 teaspoon salt
> 1 teaspoon grated orange rind

1. Melt sugar slowly in a heavy skillet, stirring constantly, until reddish brown in color. Remove from heat, and *slowly* stir in boiling water.
2. Add salt and orange rind, return to heat, and cook on medium heat until lumps are dissolved. Cool before using.

A REFRESHING SUMMER MEAL

Gazpacho
Eggplant with Rice
Sangría

This hot-weather meal features gazpacho, a cold soup, and sangría, a fruity drink.

Gazpacho

> *1/2 cup minced onion*
> *2/3 cup finely chopped cucumber*
> *1 finely chopped green pepper*
> *1 ripe avocado, diced*
> *1/2 teaspoon oregano leaves, crumbled*
> *3 tablespoons olive oil*
> *2 tablespoons wine vinegar*
> *4 cups tomato juice*
> *salt and pepper to taste*

1. Combine all ingredients, except tomato juice. Mash them with a potato masher or in a blender.
2. Add the tomato juice and chill for 1 hour. Serve with lemon or lime wedges to squeeze over soup. Top with croutons if you like. Serves 6.

Sangría

> *3 cups grape juice*
> *3 cups cranberry juice*
> *1 1/2 cups orange juice*
> *3 cups club soda*
> *3 teaspoons sugar (optional)*
> *1 orange, sliced*
> *1/2 lemon, sliced*
> *ice cubes*

1. Combine juices, club soda, and sugar in a large pitcher. Stir well.
2. Place fruit slices and ice cubes in 6 glasses.
3. Pour sangría over ice and fruit. Serves 6.

Gazpacho

Eggplant and Rice

> 3 tablespoons olive oil
> 1 onion, finely chopped
> 1 eggplant, peeled and diced
> 1 tomato, peeled and chopped
> $^1/_4$ pound fresh mushrooms, sliced
> 1 teaspoon salt
> 1 bay leaf
> $^1/_2$ teaspoon dried thyme
> 1 cup cooked rice

1. Cook the rice, following directions on the package.
2. Heat the oil in a 10-inch skillet. Add the onions and cook until soft. Add the eggplant, tomato, mushrooms, salt, bay leaf, and thyme. Sauté for 10 minutes, stirring occasionally.
3. Stir in the rice and cook until heated through. Serves 6.

A HEARTY WINTER MEAL

Green Bean Salad
Vegetable and Meat Stew
Turrones

Spicy sausages are popular throughout Spain. To make this hearty stew you can use pork sausage, Polish sausage, bratwurst, or almost any kind of sausage.

Green Bean Salad

> *1 pound fresh green beans*
> *2 cloves garlic, finely chopped*
> *1/3 cup olive oil*
> *salt to taste*

1. Wash the beans and snip off the ends with scissors. Boil beans in 2 cups of salted water until they are tender but still crisp. Drain in a colander and chill.
2. Chop the garlic, mix it with the olive oil and salt and pour this over the beans. Toss gently.
3. Arrange beans on lettuce leaves on salad plates. Serves 4.

Vegetable and Meat Stew

> *2 cups dried white or navy beans, rinsed well*
> *7 cups water*
> *1 pound spicy sausages, cut in 1-inch chunks*
> *1 medium onion, sliced*
> *4 potatoes, cubed*
> *2 green peppers, sliced*
> *2 tomatoes, cut in sections*
> *4 garlic cloves, chopped*
> *1 bay leaf*

1. Combine beans and water in a large pot. Boil for 2 minutes, then set aside for 1 hour.
2. Brown the sausage in a separate pan.

Vegetable and Meat Stew

3. After the hour is up, add the sausage, vegetables, and spices to the beans. Bring to a boil, then simmer for 2 hours, stirring frequently. Add water if the stew starts to dry out. Serve with rolls or fresh bread. Serves 4.

Turrones

> 1 pound blanched almonds
> 1 cup plus 1 tablespoon sugar
> 1/2 cup honey
> 6 tablespoons flour
> 3 tablespoons milk

1. Grease a cake pan with butter. Add the almonds. Toast in a 350° oven. Turn frequently until almonds are browned.
2. Mix the sugar, honey, and toasted almonds in a saucepan.
3. Cook on medium heat, stirring constantly, until a sticky syrup forms, then add the flour and milk. Remove from heat. Continue to stir until smooth and slightly cooled.
4. Grease an 8 x 8 inch pan with butter and coat lightly with powdered sugar. Pour mixture into pan. Cool. Cut into square pieces.

AN EVERYDAY MEAL

Spanish Omelette
Bread
Fresh Fruit

This hearty omelette contains potatoes, making it a meal in itself.

Spanish Omelette

⅓ cup olive oil, plus a little more
1 large potato, chopped
1 large onion, chopped
1 large green pepper, chopped
2 garlic cloves, minced
8 eggs, beaten
salt and pepper to taste

1. Heat the oil in a large frying pan, then add the potato, onion, garlic, and green pepper. Cook until soft.
2. Heat 1 teaspoon of oil in a small non-stick frying pan or omelette pan. Pour in ¼ of the eggs, then add ¼ of the potato, onion, and green pepper mixture.
3. As soon as eggs start to get firm, flip the omelette with a large spatula. Remove omelette when golden brown on bottom. Repeat for 3 more omelettes, keeping them warm in the oven. Serves 4.

GLOSSARY OF COOKING TERMS

For those readers who are less experienced in the kitchen, the following list explains the cooking terms used in this book.

Chopped	Cut into small pieces measuring about ½ inch thick. Finely chopped pieces should be about ⅛ inch thick.
Diced	Cut into small cubes.
Garnished	Decorated.
Grated	Cut into small pieces by using a grater.
Greased	Having been lightly coated with oil, butter, or margarine to prevent sticking.
Knead	To work dough with one's hands.
Marinate	To cover and soak with a mixture of juices, called a marinade.
Minced	Chopped into very tiny pieces.
Pinch	The amount you can pick up between your thumb and forefinger.
Reserve	To set aside an ingredient for future use.
Sauté	To cook food in oil, butter, or margarine at high temperature, while stirring constantly.
Shredded	Cut into lengths of 1–2 inches, about ¼ inch across. Finely shredded ingredients should be about ⅛ inch across.
Simmer	To cook on a stove at the lowest setting.
Sliced	Cut into thin slices that show the original shape of the object.
Toss	To mix the ingredients in a salad.
Whisk	To beat using a hand whisk or electric mixer.

SPANISH COOKING

To make the recipes in this book, you will need the following equipment and ingredients, which may not be in your kitchen:

Avocados A type of fruit that can be found in most supermarkets. When ripe they should be soft, like a ripe pear.

Blanched almonds Can be found in the baking section of a supermarket.

Garlic Fresh garlic can be found in the produce section of supermarkets. Each bulb can be broken into sections called cloves. You have to remove the brittle skin around each clove before chopping it. If you're feeling lazy, you can sometimes buy small jars of garlic that has already been chopped.

Herbs Fresh parsley and chives are usually found in the produce departments of supermarkets. Dried versions are in the spice departments.

Olive oil An oil made by pressing olives, found with other cooking oils in supermarkets.

Peppers The red, yellow, and green peppers in these recipes refer to the large "bell" peppers found in supermarkets. The red and yellow peppers are sweeter than the green ones. Some of each type make a dish very colorful!

Spices Paprika, marjoram, thyme, oregano, nutmeg, and vanilla extract can be found in the spice section of most supermarkets.

Wine vinegar This type of vinegar, made from red wine, is smoother than other vinegars.

An elegant restaurant in Barcelona is ready for hungry customers.

INDEX

We would like to thank and acknowledge the following people for the use of their photographs and transparencies:

Mark E. Ahlstrom: cover inset, 2, 9, 14, 28; Tourist Office of Spain: cover, 7, 8, 10, 11, 12, 13, 15, 16, 17, 18, 19, 21, 22, 25, 27, 30.

Produced by Mark E. Ahlstrom (The Bookworks)
Typesetting and layout by The Final Word
Photo research by Judith Ahlstrom